Hello friends... I'm Vice President Mike Pence. Welcome to this heretical coloring book that I do not endorse. I do, however, endorse Donald Trump. Together we will make my personal religious beliefs the law for all Americans, respectfully returning America to the days when men were men, women obeyed them, and children were protected from the scourge of witches and non-believers.

It's a wonderful time to be an American. Now, my dear citizens, please do your part by taking this deceitful, heathen story of Donald Trump's rise to power to your church's next book-burning ceremony.

This is Donald Trump. Color him orange. Really, really orange. You will need lots of orange because this story is all about Donald.

Let's start from the beginning. Donald was born rich: private-school-and-limousines rich.[1] Borrow-$14-million-from-your-father-to-get-started-in-life rich.[2] Donald is so rich that he was able to lose $916 million in 1995[3] and he still has enough leftover to own a private jet! This makes him a winner.

We told you Donald Trump is rich, right? Well Donald Trump wants you to know that however rich you think he is, he is even richer than that. He is so rich he lives in a tower. In fact, he owns the tower. It has many, many floors and is called Trump Tower (humble brag). Donald is the best and the richest so he lives at the top of the tower. The inside of his three-story penthouse is gold – well, gold-colored... he doesn't have quite enough money for his tower to be made of solid gold but he would like you to think he does.

1. *Confident. Incorrigible. Bully: Little Donny Was a Lot Like Candidate Donald Trump.* https://www.washingtonpost.com/lifestyle/style/young-donald-trump-military-school/2016/06/22/f0b3b164-317c-11e6-8758-d58e76e11b12_story.html

2. *Clinton Is Right About Trump's 'Very Small' $14 Million Loan.* http://www.politico.com/blogs/2016-presidential-debate-fact-check/2016/09/clinton-is-right-about-trumps-very-small-14-million-loan-228709

3. *Donald Trump Tax Records Show He Could Have Avoided Taxes for Nearly Two Decades, The* Times *Found.* http://www.nytimes.com/2016/1%2/us/politics/donald-trump-taxes.html

Donald J. Trump

These are Donald's wives – Ivana, Marla, and Melania. Donald has had three wives. They were all models or actresses when Donald met them. Donald likes models. He likes models so much that every chance he gets he trades in his wife for a younger model. That is a joke that you might not get but Donald gets it. Maybe color Donald's wives with airbrush markers. That would make sense.

Melania is Donald's current "partner for life," but Donald has a reputation to uphold – as a world-class ladies' man. Who really knows what the future could bring? Let's just go ahead and contemplate Donald's next wife. Draw what you think Donald's next wife will look like in the empty box (don't forget to give her a fun name like "Miss Teen USA"!).

1 — Ivana

2 — Marla

3 — Melania

4 —

Donald has 5 children. Donald Jr. and Eric are Donald's adult sons. For sport they hunt endangered animals in Africa.[4] Look, that's Donald Jr. with a severed elephant tail and that's Eric holding up a freshly slaughtered leopard! Donald is proud of his sons but if you are disgusted it is ok to color them with a cowardly yellow.

In the center is Donald's favorite child, Ivanka. Donald and Ivanka have a "special" relationship. In 2006, Donald told ABC's The View, "if Ivanka weren't my daughter, perhaps, I would be dating her."[5] Ivanka has been working with Donald in the family business. We aren't saying she has daddy issues, but she is a shark just like daddy. Color Ivanka gold for she truly is the Golden Child.

Donald's youngest children are Tiffany and Barron. They are young. Unlike their siblings, they don't have a public history of unsavory behavior. Yet. They probably should be left alone so maybe color them like normal people. Well, normal rich people.

* For kicks, check out the web pages showing photos that inspired the first three drawings:

- http://www.dailymail.co.uk/news/article-2114122/Donald-Eric-Trump-pictured-posing-trophy-carcasses-big-African-hunt.html

- http://www.dailymail.co.uk/femail/article-2523240/Paris-Hilton-Ivanka-Trump-post-rare-snaps-idyllic-childhoods.html

---

4. *The Trump Sons Go Hunting Again. Will More Trophy Photos Follow?* https://www.washington-post.com/news/animalia/wp/2016/08/06/the-trump-sons-go-hunting-again-will-more-trophy-photos-follow

5. *Donald Trump's Creepy Ogling of His Daughter Happened More Than You Think.* http://www.huffingtonpost.com/entry/donald-trump-ivanka-trump-comments_us_57f250d5e-4b082aad9bbf2d7

Donald Jr.

Eric

Ivanka (w/Daddy)

Tiffany

Barron

Now that you've colored Donald's "colorful" family it's time to take a closer look at Donald – a man who has done it all.

Donald has sold steaks.[6] Donald has opened a university. Donald has closed a university.[7,8] Donald has built luxury golf courses.[9] Donald has stiffed general contractors and service providers.[10] Donald has sued people and been sued by people.[11] Donald has owned the Miss Universe pageant.[12] Donald has attacked, punched, and shaved Vince McMahon at Wrestlemania 23![13] Donald is living the American Dream! Well, his version of the American Dream.

Donald's life could hardly get any better. Or could it? It totally could. In 2004, Donald got his very own tv show! With cameras and everything. Donald's tv show was no ordinary tv show. It was a REALITY tv show and that's the best kind. Donald's show was called The Apprentice. Donald got famous for sitting in a board room and saying, "You're Fired!"[14] It's a catchy line. Maybe try yelling it out at your place of work and see how things go for you. Just kidding, don't do that. This catch phrase is really only for Donald.

6. *Trump Steaks, Wine, Water: Why Donald Doesn't Own Most of Those Products.* http://www.npr.org/2016/03/09/469836959/trump-steaks-wine-water-why-donald-doesnt-own-most-of-those-products

7. *Trump University: It's Worse Than You Think.* http://www.newyorker.com/news/john-cassidy/trump-university-its-worse-than-you-think

8. *Donald Trump Agrees to Pay $25 Million in Trump University Settlement.* http://www.nytimes.com/2016/11/19/us/politics/trump-university.html?_r=0

9. *Taxpayers Built This New York Golf Course. Trump Reaps the Rewards.* https://www.washingtonpost.com/news/business/wp/2016/08/25/taxpayers-built-this-new-york-golf-course-trump-reaps-the-rewards

10. *USA Today Exclusive: Hundreds Allege Donald Trump Doesn't Pay His Bills.* http://www.usatoday.com/story/news/politics/elections/2016/06/09/donald-trump-unpaid-bills-republican-president-laswuits/85297274

11. *Donald Trump: Three Decades, 4,095 Lawsuits.* http://www.usatoday.com/pages/interactives/trump-lawsuits

12. *A Timeline of Donald Trump's Creepiness While He Owned Miss Universe.* http://www.rollingstone.com/politics/features/timeline-of-trumps-creepiness-while-he-owned-miss-universe-w444634

13. *Donald Trump and WWE: How the Road to the White House Began at 'WrestleMania'.* http://www.rollingstone.com/sports/features/donald-trump-and-wwe-how-the-road-to-the-white-house-began-at-wrestlemania-20160201

14. *The Inside Story of How 'The Apprentice' Rescued Donald Trump.* http://fortune.com/2016/09/08/donald-trump-the-apprentice-burnett

Being on tv pleased Donald very much. All that attention! And Donald is quite the entertainer. Donald says all sorts of entertaining things. Like in 2011, when Donald said this about President Barack Obama: "I'm starting to think that he was not born here."[15] That's pretty funny, isn't it? Donald got lots of attention spreading Birther conspiracies. Gossip, gossip, gossip. Oh Donald, you should totally get into politics. You are so good at it.

Donald must have read our minds because he *did* get into politics. Of course, we were just joking when we suggested it. But Donald didn't get the joke. Instead he announced he would be running for president... of the United States. Donald didn't have many supporters at this time. In fact, the day Donald announced his candidacy there was an ad offering movie extras $50 to help fill the room.[16] They held up signs and applauded the idea of Donald Trump as president of the United States.

On that day a ~~fraud~~ star was born!

* Candidacy announcement transcript can be seen at: https://www.washingtonpost. com/news/post-politics/wp/2015/06/16/ full-text-donald-trump-announces-a-presidential-bid/?utm_term=.b08acb0d03f5

15. *Donald Trump Clung to 'Birther' Lie for Years, and Still Isn't Apologetic.* http://www.nytimes. com/2016/09/17/us/politics/donald-trump-obama-birther.html

16. *Donald Trump Reportedly Paid Actors $50 to Cheer for Him at His 2016 Announcement.* http:// www.businessinsider.com/paid-actors-at-donald-trump-announcement-2015-6

If Donald wanted to be the president he must first win the GOP nomination. He faced some formidable opponents. Donald would need to be a Grade-A Alpha Male to dominate this group. He came up with clever nicknames for his opponents to show everyone how presidential he was. There was "Lyin' Ted," "Little Marco," and "Low-Energy Jeb." Donald was a bold truth-teller. He wasn't afraid of telling Republican primary voters what they needed to hear – that there was "no problem" with his hand size and so he did not have a wee wee-wee.[17] This was going to be a campaign of ~~great new ideas~~ "epic proportions"! The Republican Party had found their candidate.·

---

17. *Donald Trump Defends Size of His Penis.* http://www.cnn.com/2016/03/03/politics/donald-trump-small-hands-marco-rubio

Donald was the GOP nominee. It was time to have a party! Donald and his followers got their American flag on in Cleveland, Ohio at the Republican National Convention. Donald's party was kind of a ~~dark and depressing~~ "non-traditional" affair. None of the regular party-goers were in attendance. In fact, no former presidents or GOP nominees came to Donald's party.[18] But Donald's children were there and Melania was there. In fact, Melania made headlines with her big speech. We later found out that part of her speech was actually taken from a speech given by Michele Obama[19] but doesn't Melania look beautiful on stage? She glows like an angel – a beautiful, plagiarizing angel.

Inspired by his super successful party (the best!), Donald set out his bold new agenda for the American people. Tax cuts for the wealthy (no matter the deficit)! New jobs in dirty fossil fuels (no matter the cost to the environment)! An anti-choice Supreme Court (no matter that Constitutional rights also apply to women)! All popular ideas – propping up the rich, destroying the earth, denying women basic human rights – with a sure-fire plan like this, we'd like to see him lose!

---

18. *Dumpster Fires, Fishing and Travel: These Republicans Are Sitting out the RNC.* http://www.npr.org/2016/07/18/486398726/dumpster-fires-fishing-and-travel-these-republicans-are-sitting-out-the-rnc

19. *RNC Official Cites 'My Little Pony' to Defend Melania Trump.* http://www.cnn.com/2016/07/19/politics/sean-spicer-melania-trump-my-little-pony

Donald's "can-destroy" attitude was starting to catch on! Donald was winning the hearts and minds of everyday Americans 140 characters at a time. That's right, Donald tweets. In fact, Donald is so good at tweeting that he once tweeted: "Thanks- many are saying I'm the best 140 character writer in the world. It's easy when it's fun."[20] And Donald was having lots of fun. Don't you think it makes Donald seem presidential when he tweets: "boring," "crooked," "arrogant," "nasty," and "total disaster" at members of the press, world leaders, and political opponents? (Hint: you better answer this question with a resounding "yes" before Donald finds out and labels you "really pathetic," "phony," "low energy," "weak," or "a loser"!)[21]

---

20. *Donald Trump's Most Outrageous Tweets of All Time.* http://mashable.com/2016/03/21/donald-trump-best-tweets/#oOZLGRipLsqG

21. *The 282 People, Places and Things Donald Trump Has Insulted on Twitter: A Complete List.* http://www.nytimes.com/interactive/2016/0½8/upshot/donald-trump-twitter-insults.html?_r=0

Donald felt his Twitter feed told Americans all they needed to know. Still, many Americans wanted to see Donald's tax returns. This hurt Donald's feelings. Why would people not trust Donald's word about his past financial dealings and ties to foreign nations?[22]

Since we may never get to see Donald's actual tax returns here is a blank, imaginary tax return. Please fill it in for Donald however you like. Don't be shy! This is a place to show off your creativity. Just think of all the ~~illegal or unscrupulous~~ amazingly successful financial details Donald could be so modestly hiding and put them to paper. Who knows – you could be right about *any* of it or *all* of it!

* See item 22 from the July 20, 2015 Washington Post article: https://www. washingtonpost.com/news/the-fix/ wp/2015/07/20/25-people-places-and-things-donald-trump-has-denounced/?utm_ term=.62f1cb05106a

22. *Donald Trump's Tax Returns: Why Won't He Release Them?* http://www.cnn.com/2016/09/07/politics/donald-trump-tax-audit-tax-returns

Form 1040-R

Department of the Treasury—Internal Revenue Service

U.S. Individual Income Tax Return for the Rich

First Name: Donald J.	Last Name: Trump	Social Security Number
Home Address		☐ Presidential Election Campaign
City, Town, State, and Zip		Check here if you want to become President to enrich yourself at the expense of America

Filing Status			
	1 ☐ Bigly-Rich	3 ☐ Uber-Rich	5 ☐ Yuuuge-Rich
	2 ☐ Mega-Rich	4 ☐ Wicked-Rich	6 ☐ Psychopath

Exemptions			
	7a ☐ Yourself	7b ☐ Trophy Wife	7c ☐ Trust-Fund Babies:
	Trust Fund Baby 1:	Trust Fund Baby 2:	Trust Fund Baby 3:

Income	Attach an additional page if the number of digits overflows the field	
Attach Form(s) (If you feel like it)	**8a** Amount of income you bragged about to your wealthy friends	
	8b Actual amount of income	
	9a Amount you falsely pledged to charity	
	9b Amount you actually gave to charity	
	9c Value of things you bought for yourself with your own foundation's income	
	10a Amount of income you told the voting public you received from Russia	
	10b Actual amount of income you received from Russia	
Tax and Credits	**11** Itemized Deductions	
	12 Exemptions	
	13 Tax (You will only have to pay this if you are stupid, which you are not because you are rich. See instructions.)	
	If you are so good at business that you had more losses than profits, enter your losses here. This may get you out of paying taxes for many, many years	
Refund	Again, you may need to attach an additional page if the number of digits overflows the space allotted in the field	
Amount You Owe	Just kidding! You must be thinking of Form 1040 for schmucks. This is 1040-R for the rich!	

Sign Here ▶	Your signature	Date
	Your occupation	☐ Check if you've never actually worked

Paid Preparer ▶	Name	Date
	Signature	☐ Check if you wear a yarmulke*

Donald was sad about all those questions about his taxes. Questions, questions, questions. He needed to distract the American people so they would stop pestering him about his possible conflicts of interest.[23] It was time for him to return to a campaign of baseless fear!

Donald got a lot of attention for painting illegal immigrants from Mexico as murderers and rapists. Donald soon discovered that not only could he create a phony racially-based problem but he could solve it, too!

"BUILD THAT WALL!"

Donald's 30- or 50-foot high concrete wall[24] on the border with Mexico would keep out those pesky brown-rapist-immigrants.[25] And Donald was going to make Mexico pay for the wall! Donald must have been pretty bummed when former Mexican President Felipe Calderon said, "we are not going to pay any single cent for such a stupid wall! And it's going to be completely useless."[26]

When Donald gets his wall Felipe is not going to be allowed to visit!

---

23. *Donald Trump's Many, Many, Many, Many Conflicts of Interest.* http://time.com/4574938/donald-trump-conflicts-of-interest

24. *Donald Trump's Mexico Border Wall Will Be as High as 55 feet, According to Donald Trump.* https://www.washingtonpost.com/news/the-fix/wp/2016/02/26/so-how-high-will-donald-trumps-wall-be-an-investigation

25. *'Totally Accurate': Trump Defends Calling Mexican Immigrants 'Rapists'.* http://www.msnbc.com/msnbc/totally-accurate-trump-defends-calling-mexican-immigrants-rapists

26. *Mexico Won't Pay a Cent for Trump's 'Stupid Wall'.* http://www.cnbc.com/2016/02/08/mexico-wont-pay-single-cent-for-trumps-stupid-wall.html

Donald was back on track! He had found his racist jam and now he could focus on taking down his political opponent. That would be the Democratic Party nominee Hillary Clinton.

This is Hillary Clinton. She is a smart lady with lots of innovative ideas for America.[27] Hillary is what we might call a policy wonk.[28] She has been working on public policy for most of her life. Work, work, work. Donald didn't like the idea of this campaign being about public policy. Donald wanted this campaign to be about words. So he came up with a few for Hillary and repeated them over and over again: "devil",[29] "crooked",[30] "world class liar".[31]

Bummer for Hillary – she brought a calculator to a knife fight. So many bold ideas from such a "nasty woman"!

---

27. *Learn More About Hillary's Vision for America.* https://www.hillaryclinton.com/issues

28. *Hillary Clinton Has a Very Detailed Plan for the Economy. That May Be a Problem.* https://www.washingtonpost.com/news/wonk/wp/2016/07/29/hillary-clinton-has-a-very-detailed-plan-for-the-economy-that-may-be-a-problem

29. *Donald Trump Calls Hillary Clinton 'The Devil'.* http://abcnews.go.com/Politics/donald-trump-calls-hillary-clinton-devil/story?id=41056426

30. *Donald Trump Has Come up With His Clinton Nickname: 'Crooked Hillary'.* https://newrepublic.com/minutes/132765/donald-trump-come-clinton-nickname-crooked-hillary

31. *Trump, in Speech, Attacks Clinton as 'World-Class Liar'.* http://www.politico.com/story/2016/06/trump-clinton-is-a-world-class-liar-224653

Donald was pretty good at making up stuff about Hillary.[32] His words were really starting to stick. Donald was also pretty good at being a bully. Bully Hillary. Bully the press. Bully anyone who asked him a question he didn't know the answer to. Donald was a natural. He had been bullying people his entire life. Things were rolling along for Donald's campaign, when he suddenly got hit by a bus. Well not literally. There was a bus but rather than get hit by it Donald was on it. Donald was on it saying all sorts of ~~lecherous and predatory~~ "interesting" things with Billy Bush. Donald was bragging about trying to cheat on his wife. Donald was boasting about assaulting women and getting away with it because he was a celebrity![33]

Whew, Donald was in a tough spot. A ~~better~~ lesser man would have sincerely apologized and dropped out of the race. But not Donald. Donald was in it to win it, and a little "locker room talk" wasn't going to stop him now.

You might be wondering what Donald will feel entitled to do to women once he is in charge of the free world. Good news! Now you don't have to wonder because Donald told you what he'll do.

* Actual transcript from conversation on Access Hollywood bus between Donald Trump and Billy Bush in 2005.[33]

32. *Hillary Clinton Drops a Debate Bomb on Trump by Releasing 19 Pages Of His Fact Checked Lies.* http://www.politicususa.com/2016/09/23/hillary-clinton-drops-debate-bomb-trump-releasing-19-pages-fact-checked-lies.html

33. *Transcript: Donald Trump's Taped Comments About Women.* http://www.nytimes.com/2016/1%8/us/donald-trump-tape-transcript.html

Donald was in a tough spot. He was going to need some friends to help Americans forget that he bragged about assaulting women. Political friends are sometimes called surrogates. Donald has had lots of surrogates. Let's take a look at some.

First is New Jersey Governor Chris Christie. Chris wasn't always a big fan of Donald's. In fact, Chris once called Donald a "carnival barker."[34] We don't even know what that means but it sure doesn't sound like Chris and Donald are friends. Chris doesn't know it yet but once the campaign is over Donald is going to drop him faster than a wife pushing forty! And, it is probably for the best since Chris is potentially in big trouble for his role seeking political revenge against a New Jersey mayor who didn't support Chris when he was running for governor.[35]

Donald also has former New York City Mayor Rudy Giuliani as his surrogate. We wonder, does Donald know that Rudy used taxpayer money to visit his mistress in the Hamptons?[36] Donald likes Rudy because Rudy is good at talking. Talk, talk, talk. You can ask Rudy about Donald's latest lies and he will tell you that Hillary is the worst, just the worst. What Rudy says usually doesn't make much sense but he says it louder and for longer than you can stand to listen. You can see how Donald would like this guy!

* From Lewis Carroll's *Through the Looking Glass*

34. *What Chris Christie Said About Donald Trump BEFORE the Endorsement.* http://talkingpointsmemo.com/dc/christie-past-comments-trump

35. *Bridgegate: Questions on Christie Role Swirl After Ex-Allies' Conviction.* http://www.chicagotribune.com/news/nationworld/ct-new-jersey-bridge-trial-verdict-20161104-story.html

36. *Giuliani Billed Obscure Agencies for Trips.* http://www.politico.com/story/2007/11/giuliani-billed-obscure-agencies-for-trips-007073

Donald's also got the best campaign manager – Kellyanne Conway. She has a heart of gold and spins like a top. This is a metaphor. Do you get it? Kellyanne will tell you that Hillary Clinton "might" be indicted on felony charges when she knows it isn't happening. She'll tell you that it doesn't matter if information is true, it only matters if voters *think* it is true. If you pay Kellyanne enough money she'll say anything you tell her to say. In fact, she used to say some really bad things about Donald. She called him "unpresidential" and "vulgar" and accused him of building his business on the back of the little guy.

Donald can recognize a nihilistic fraud when he sees one. He figured out that if he gave Kellyanne enough money she would say horrible things about *other* people instead of him![37] Usually Donald doesn't like paying people who work for him,[38] but Donald thinks that Kellyanne Conway has been worth the money.

Let's pretend Kellyanne is on your payroll. Fill in Kellyanne's empty speech bubble with whatever you want – remember, for cash she'll say just about *anything*!

---

37. *Here's How Trump's New Campaign Manager Attacked Him as a Cable News Pundit.* http://media-matters.org/research/2016/08/19/here-s-how-trump-s-new-campaign-manager-attacked-him-cable-news-pundit/212524

38. *One Secret of Trump's Low-Cost Campaign: Free Labor.* http://www.reuters.com/article/us-usa-election-trump-staff-idUSKCN1181CV

Donald's such a swell guy, he's got friends and surrogates all around the world. For example, Donald is friends with Vladimir Putin ("Pootie"). Pootie is a dictator. Pootie imprisons and kills his political enemies in Russia and throughout the world.[39] Pootie doesn't like free speech or free press. He would hate our First Amendment. (He does like fake news though!)[40] Pootie and Donald are friends. And friends help out their friends. That's why Pootie hacked the private email accounts of Hillary Clinton's aide and the Democratic National Committee and released their emails to the public. Pootie wanted to undermine democracy in the United States and help his friend Donald win the election.[41,42,43] Then it's back to the hard work of murdering civilian women, men and children in Syria![44]

* Donald Trump's actual response to Hillary Clinton during a presidential debate on Oct 19, 2016. See transcript at http://www.nytimes.com/2016/10/20/us/politics/third-debate-transcript.html

39. *More of Kremlin's Opponents Are Ending up Dead.* http://www.nytimes.com/2016/08/21/world/europe/moscow-kremlin-silence-critics-poison.html

40. *Russian Propaganda Effort Helped Spread 'Fake News' During Election, Experts Say.* https://www.washingtonpost.com/business/economy/russian-propaganda-effort-helped-spread-fake-news-during-election-experts-say/2016/1¼/793903b6-8a40-4ca9-b712-716af66098fe_story.html?tid=a_inl&utm_term=.b0115171cb0a

41. *Putin and Russia's Main Target in U.S. Election: Democracy.* http://www.cbsnews.com/news/putin-and-russias-main-target-in-us-election-democracy

42. *Here's What You Need to Know About Russia's Election Hacking so Far.* https://www.washingtonpost.com/news/post-nation/wp/2016/12/14/heres-what-you-need-to-know-about-the-cias-assessment-into-russia-hacking-so-far/?utm_term=.d5e6755ace13

43. *FBI in Agreement With CIA That Russia Aimed to Help Trump Win White House.* https://www.washingtonpost.com/world/national-security/fbi-backs-cia-view-that-russia-intervened-to-help-trump-win-election/2016/12/16/05b42c0e-c3bf-11e6-9a51-cd56ea1c2bb7_story.html

44. *Russia Has Killed More Civilians in Syria Than ISIS: Human Rights Report.* http://dailycaller.com/2016/08/19/russia-has-killed-more-civilians-in-syria-than-isis-human-rights-report

Donald is proud of his political allies but he'd get nowhere without a solid group of supporters. And Donald's got a great flock. He can retweet White Supremacist nonsense and they are *still* on board with him.[45] They just want to "Make America Great Again" and they are getting started right away! Some of Donald's choicest supporters have shown up at his rallies chanting "Build a Wall – Kill Them All!"[46], "Lock Her Up!"[47] and "Jew-S-A!"[48] They've been threatening the press with swastikas[49] and spreading fake news stories on Facebook and Twitter.[50]

Donald's minions were everywhere – shouting from the back of their Confederate flag-decorated pickups and trolling the media from their laptops in American hotbeds like Russia and Macedonia!

45. *His Racism Is No Accident: Trump Has Retweeted White Supremacists 75 Times.* http://www.politicususa.com/2016/07/03/proof-racism-accidenttrump-retweeted-white-suprema-cists-75-times.html

46. *Voices From Donald Trump's Rallies, Uncensored.* http://www.nytimes.com/2016/08/04/politics/donald-trump-supporters.html

47. *A Brief History of the 'Lock Her Up!' Chant by Trump Supporters Against Clinton.* https://www.washingtonpost.com/news/the-fix/wp/2016/1½2/a-brief-history-of-the-lock-her-up-chant-as-it-looks-like-trump-might-not-even-try

48. *'Jew-S-A!' Chant Is Latest Reminder of White Supremacist Support for Trump.* https://www.washingtonpost.com/politics/trump-campaign-manager-condemns-rally-supporter-who-chanted-jew-s-a/2016/10/30/92e73622-9ee2-11e6-8832-23a007c77bb4_story.html

49. *Swastika Sign Left on Press Table After Trump Rally.* http://www.cnn.com/videos/politics/2016/10/13/donald-trump-rally-swastika-media-sign-acosta-tsr-sot.cnn

50. *Facebook Fake-News Writer: 'I Think Donald Trump Is in the White House Because of Me'.* https://www.washingtonpost.com/news/the-intersect/wp/2016/11/17/facebook-fake-news-writer-i-think-donald-trump-is-in-the-white-house-because-of-me

Donald had made it to late October but things weren't looking very good. He was losing this campaign... big league. Pootie and Donald's friends in the media had helped some, but Donald needed to catch another break.

Who's that? ~~Republican agent~~ FBI Director James Comey?!?

And what is he doing in the closing days of the 2016 election?!?

Why, James Comey is dropping a bombshell on Donald's opponent, Hillary Clinton. This is another metaphor. Comey didn't literally bomb Hillary. That would be wrong. He just "blew up" Hillary's campaign, seemingly swaying voters toward supporting Donald Trump.[51,52] Comey started gossip that Hillary *may* have done something illegal 4-8 years ago and he was maybe going to file charges against her. Of course she hadn't and he didn't but Donald had a lie to sell to the American people and he was going to sell it like candy at Halloween![53]

* Comey's full letter can be seen at: http://www.businessinsider.com/fbi-re-opening-investigation-into-hillary-private-e-mail-server-2016-10

51. *It's Hard to See How James Comey Could Have Handled This Last 9 Days any Worse.* https://www.washingtonpost.com/news/the-fix/wp/2016/11/06/james-comey-totally-botched-the-last-10-days-of-the-2016-election

52. *How Much Did Comey Hurt Clinton's Chances?* https://fivethirtyeight.com/features/how-much-did-comey-hurt-clintons-chances

53. *Comey's Letter May Be too Little too Late.* http://www.cnn.com/2016/11/06/politics/james-comey-fbi-hillary-clinton

Election Day was here: November 8, 2016. Donald was within the polling margin of error! Donald's Republican friends had done their part. Donald had done his part. Election returns slowly turned Donald's presidential candidacy into a reality.[54] Donald couldn't believe it! He hadn't even wanted to be president! Donald was just hoping to sell his brand and now he was president-elect of the United States of America. Hallelujah, he and his whole family could make even more money for themselves!

Donald has reached the mountaintop but many Americans are afraid of what kind of America he sees from up there. This is no longer Donald Trump's story. This is our story. Take a look at these Americans. There are men and women, and people of various races, incomes, orientations and abilities. The majority of these Americans did not vote for Donald Trump.[55]

Color these Americans however you like – this is still America, and this is *your* coloring book!

---

54. *Election Results.* https://elections16.usatoday.com/results/president

55. *Clinton Won as Many Votes as Obama in 2012 — Just Not in the States Where She Needed Them Most.* http://www.latimes.com/politics/la-na-pol-election-final-20161209-story.html

I'm worried that Trump's fragile ego and avarice will send us off to war for no good reason.

I'm concerned about respect for science, the environment and the future of this planet for my kids.

I'm afraid that Trump's judicial appointees will undo the legal progress of the last 50 years.

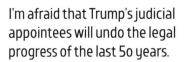

I'm concerned Trump's policies will lower wages and increase the deficit.

I'm wondering if Trump and his cabinet will serve all Americans, or just their rich cronies.

I want to know that the feds will work with us, not against us, to keep our communities safe.

I'm not worried, I'm ready to fight! We won't let these crooks take away our rights!

I'm afraid that fewer Americans will be able to have health insurance under Trump's plans.

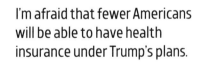

I'm terrified that Trump's arrogance and ignorance will get us all nuked. Literally.

Epilogue

We watched events unfold in the 2016 election season with fear, sadness, and disbelief. Like many Americans, we were disturbed that Donald Trump emerged as the Republican nominee. Donald Trump was not just unapologetic but proud of his misogynistic and bigoted remarks and actions. He was grossly unqualified to be president, yet the Republican Party gave him a home and a platform for his discourse. So far the presidency is shaping up to be even more "colorful" than the campaign.

We understand if this coloring book hasn't made you feel all the way better about the news being generated daily by the White House's ongoing fiascos. Got some complaints? Need to get them off your chest? Try petitioning "the gov" for a redress of grievances. In case you don't have these numbers on speed dial or these websites bookmarked, we offer them for your convenience:

U.S. Capitol Switchboard

(202) 224-3121

White House Comments

(202) 456-1111

White House Contact

https://www.whitehouse.gov/contact

Petition the White House

https://petitions.whitehouse.gov

About Us

Following the election, we wanted to do something to help assuage our angst. We thought the coloring book would be an entertaining way to simultaneously offer some meditative relief while documenting what Donald Trump got away with in 2016. This project was for us but we wanted to share it with all of you.

Megan Ferrell (author)

Megan is a web developer in Portland, Oregon. She enjoys good political satire such as Full Frontal, the former Colbert Report and, of course, Fox News. Her likes include animals (most especially marmots), the outdoors (most especially the High Sierras), American history, and civility. Her dislikes include littering, cilantro, and mean people.

Nicole Aue (illustrator)

Nicole is a graphic designer and ux/web designer from Portland, Oregon. She is a life-long fan of comic books and the unique avenue of storytelling they provide. She enjoys playing outside, asking questions, learning new stuff, solving puzzles, and generally being a total hermit. You cannot connect with her on social media because she hates it (in a nice way).

First published in the United States of
America in 2017 in Portland, Oregon.

All contents, text and illustration
copyright ©2017 by 45th Parallel Design, LLC.

https://www.colorustrumped.com

Author: Megan Ferrell

Designer / Illustrator: Nicole Aue